EXCELLENCE IN HIGHER EDUCATION WORKBOOK AND SCORING INSTRUCTIONS

Available Companion Volumes

Excellence in Higher Education Guide

This new (8th) edition of the *Excellence in Higher Education Guide* updates and extends this classic work. This edition includes a broad and integrated approach to the design, assessment, planning, and improvement of colleges and universities of all types, as well as individual academic, student affairs, administrative, and services units. The framework is adaptable to institutions and units with any mission and is consistent with the current directions within regional and programmatic accreditation.

Excellence in Higher Education: Facilitator's Materials

This e-book is intended for those leading an EHE program, allowing facilitators to customize the EHE materials and adapt exercises to the needs of particular organizations.

Excellence in Higher Education Guide & Facilitator's Materials Set

This package consists of a paperback copy of the *Excellence in Higher Education Guide* and the *Excellence in Higher Education: Facilitator's Materials* e-book.

EXCELLENCE IN HIGHER EDUCATION WORKBOOK AND SCORING INSTRUCTIONS

A Framework for the Design, Assessment, and Continuous Improvement of Institutions, Departments, and Programs

8th Edition

Brent D. Ruben

Routledge
Taylor & Francis Group

NEW YORK AND LONDON

First published 2016 by Stylus Publishing, LLC

Published 2023 by Routledge
605 Third Avenue, New York, NY 10017
4 Park Square, Milton Park, Abingdon, Oxon OX14 4RN

Routledge is an imprint of the Taylor & Francis Group, an informa business

For information on programs, materials, or use of *Excellence in Higher Education Guide: A Framework for the Design, Assessment, and Continuous Improvement of Institutions, Departments, and Programs, Eighth Edition,* contact Brent D. Ruben, 2 Regina Drive, Hillsborough, NJ, 08844, e-mail: bruben@rutgers.edu.

ISBN 13: 978-1-62036-400-0 (pbk)
ISBN 13: 978-1-00-344468-8 (ebk)

DOI: 10.4324/9781003444688

Contents

Workbook and Scoring Instructions

Excellence in Higher Education Guide
8th Edition

Brent D. Ruben, PhD
Rutgers University

A Rubric for Designing, Assessing, and Improving a Higher Education Institution, Department, or Program

1. Defines **standards** of excellence and effectiveness based on the mission and aspirations of an institution and its academic, administrative, student life, and service departments and their programs and services

2. Provides **a strategy** for highlighting current strengths and areas in need of change

3. Serves as **a tool** to inventory, organize, and integrate existing assessment, planning, improvement, and other change initiatives

4. Offers **a blueprint** for designing new or reorganized institutions, departments, programs, or services

EHE Resources

- 8th edition of the *Guide*

Plus 8th editions of

- *Workbook and Scoring Instructions*
- *Facilitator's Materials*

Core Principles and Values

- Clear and shared sense of purpose (mission) and future aspirations (vision)

- Effective leadership and governance processes

- Active engagement of faculty, staff, and other critical stakeholders in planning

- Strong and reciprocally valued relationships among faculty, staff, and external constituencies

- Pursuit of high standards and innovation in programs and services

- Qualified and dedicated faculty and staff, effective organizational structures, and a satisfying workplace climate

- Consideration of approach, implementation, and results

- Commitment to tracking outcomes, ongoing review, improvement, and innovation in all areas

Similarities Among Baldrige, EHE, and Accreditation

All emphasize:

- Expansive view of excellence
- Leadership and planning
- Clear, shared, and measurable goals
- Focus on faculty, staff, students, and other external constituencies
- Systematic assessment of the effectiveness of the institution or organization as a whole, as well as the effectiveness of specific programs, services, and other organizational activities and functions
- Comparisons with peers and leaders
- Focus on outcomes
- Iterative cycles of review, planning, and continuous improvement

Common Themes

CORE PRINCIPLES OF BALDRIGE-BASED AND ACCREDITATION FRAMEWORKS

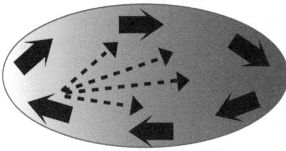

Development and Review of the
Mission and Vision of the Institution,
Department, or Program

Improvement,
Innovation,
Reinvention,
or Elimination

Establishment of
Goals

Assessment of
Outcomes

Design of Programs
and Services

Delivery of Programs
and Services

EHE: A Flexible, Scalable, and Integrating Framework

- Useful for academic, student life, service, and administrative organizations
- Appropriate for departments, programs, centers, advisory councils, governing groups of any size, or an entire institution
- Integrates Baldrige and accreditation frameworks and standards and uses the language of higher education
- Built around widely accepted standards of organizational effectiveness
- Inventories and integrates ongoing assessment, planning, and improvement initiatives
- Facilitates systematic review and creates baseline measures
- Provides a language for information and best practices sharing across institutions, departments, and programs
- Broadens participation in leadership and problem solving

Levels of Assessment, Planning, and Improvement

- System
- Institution
- Department
- Program

The EHE framework consists of **seven categories or themes** critical to the effectiveness of any educational institution, department, or program.

The categories are viewed as distinct but interrelated components of any higher education organization.

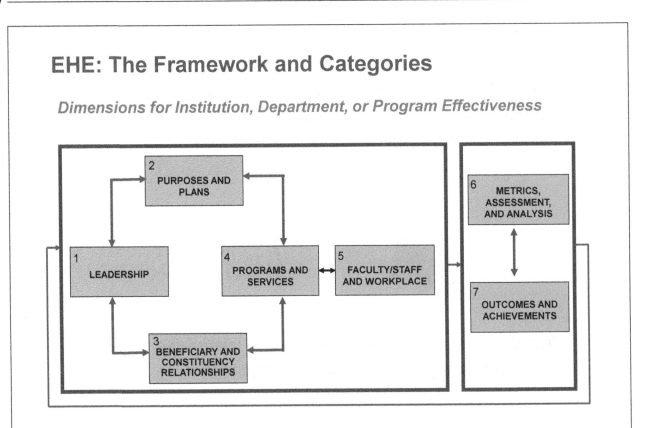

EHE: The Framework and Categories

Dimensions for Institution, Department, or Program Effectiveness

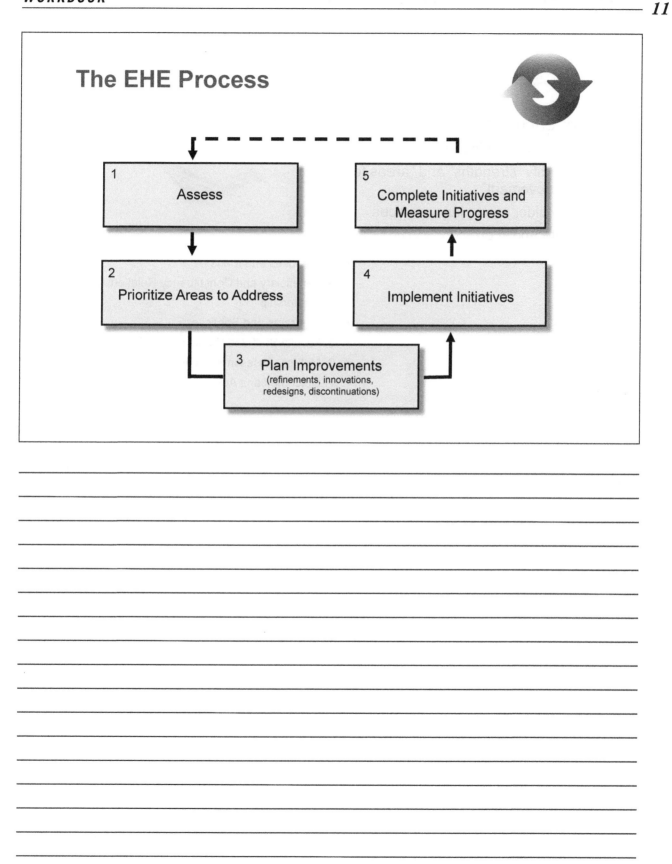

The EHE Process

1 Assess

2 Prioritize Areas to Address

3 Plan Improvements
(refinements, innovations, redesigns, discontinuations)

4 Implement Initiatives

5 Complete Initiatives and Measure Progress

Steps in the EHE Self-Assessment Process

For each category:

- Review and discuss
- Identify "strengths" and "areas for improvement"
- Consider exemplary practices
- Rate and score

- ✓ 2: Purposes and Plans
- ✓ 3: Beneficiary and Constituency Relationships
- ✓ 1: Leadership
- ✓ 4: Programs and Services
- ✓ 5: Faculty/Staff and Workplace
- ✓ 6: Metrics, Assessment, and Analysis
- ✓ 7: Outcomes and Achievements

_____
_____
_____
_____
_____
_____
_____
_____
_____
_____
_____
_____
_____
_____
_____
_____
_____

For Each Category

STRENGTHS	AREAS FOR IMPROVEMENT

Percentage Rating Guide Summary

Rating	Approach and Implementation in
90% – 100%	ALL
70% – 80%	MOST
50% – 60%	MANY
30% – 40%	SOME
10% – 20%	A FEW
0%	NO systematic approach or implementation; not part of culture

- Areas, programs, services
- Parts of the culture
- Beneficiary and constituency groups

A Sample Rating Summary

Rating

0%	10%	20%	30%	40%	50%	60%	70%	80%	90%	100%
		3	5	4	1					
		60	150	160	50					

$$\underline{420} \quad / \quad \underline{13} \quad = \quad \underline{\mathbf{32.31 = 32\%}}$$

Weighted   Number   **Average Rating**
Total*   Voting   **(Average %)**

* The *weighted total* is the number of tallies in each column multiplied by the respective percentage score and summed across the columns.

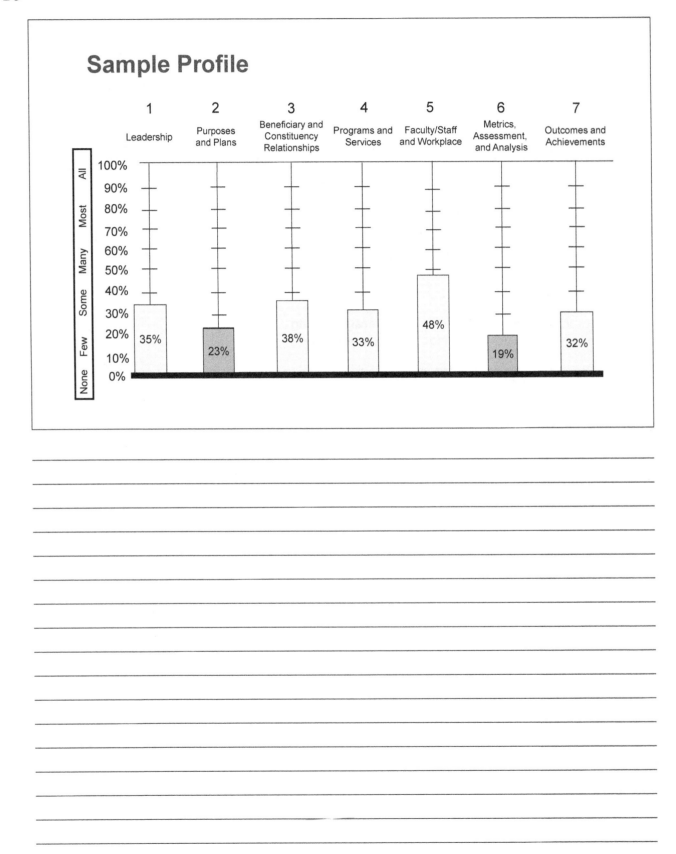

Category 2: Purposes and Plans: Establishing and Pursuing Shared Aims

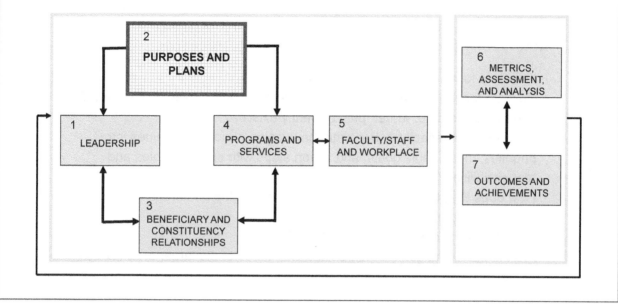

Category 2: Purposes and Plans

This category focuses on the planning process and how the organization's mission, aspirations, and values are developed and communicated; how they are translated into goals and action steps and coordinated throughout the organization; and how faculty and staff are engaged in these processes.

- Is there a formalized planning process?
- How are faculty and staff engaged in developing and implementing plans?
- Does an up-to-date, written plan currently exist?
- Does that plan effectively translate the mission, vision, and values into priorities, measurable goals, and action steps with specified roles and responsibilities?
- How does the plan take account of current strengths and areas in need of improvement, innovation, or elimination?
- Does the plan consider resource needs?
- Are the plans and goals synchronized with those of the larger organization or institution?

Strategic Planning in Higher Education

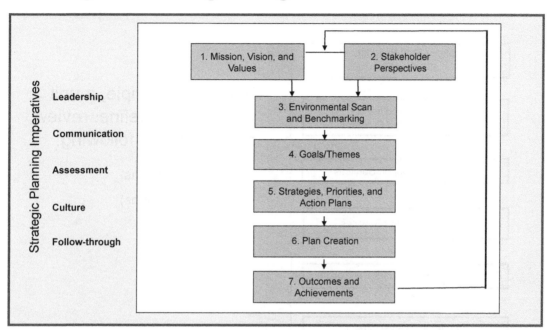

Note. Based on Tromp, P., & Ruben, B. (2010). *Strategic Planning in Higher Education: A Guide for Leaders.* Washington, DC: National Association of College and University Business Officers.

Examples

Faculty or Staff Recruitment and Welcome

Orientation to Requirements and Programs

Instructional Support Services

Research Support Services

Faculty or Staff Professional Development

Leadership Development

For each example, a unit may elect to define, review, and clarify the following:

- Purposes (Missions)
- Aspirations (Visions)
- Plans
- Goals
- Strategies

Purposes and Plans

Exemplary Practices

- A clear and shared sense of the organization's purpose and aspirations
- A formal planning process in place and understood by all
- Plans fully synchronized with the mission, vision, and values of the organization *and* institution
- Plans include short- and long-term goals
- Sufficient time and resources allocated for benchmarking and peer-review research, environmental scanning, and the development and pilot testing of innovations
- Plans include clear, measurable, and ambitious goals and action steps and a strategy for monitoring progress to completion
- Plans identify possible programs and services that should be improved and also programs and services that are candidates for major renovation or discontinuation
- Resources, climate, culture, and peer comparisons integral to the planning process
- Plans anticipate and address strategic opportunities and unexpected events and "crises"
- Plans, goals, and action plans broadly communicated and enthusiastically supported and pursued throughout the organization

2: Purposes and Plans

STRENGTHS	AREAS FOR IMPROVEMENT

The Rating Process

Consider:

❑ *Approach*: Methods and strategies

❑ *Implementation*: The way approaches are put into practice

- Are all aspects of the category addressed?

- To what extent are the approach and implementation efforts
    - Effective?
    - Systematic?
    - Integrated?
    - Consistently applied?
    - In place in all areas of the organization?
    - Regularly reviewed and improved?

(Nothing in Place) 0%   50%   100% (The Best Anywhere)

Percentage Rating Guide

Rating	Approach and Implementation
100% to 90%	• A superior approach, systematically addressing **all** dimensions of the category • **Fully** implemented without significant weakness or gaps in any area • Widely recognized leader in the category or item • Systematic approach and commitment to excellence and continuous improvement **fully** ingrained in the organization and its culture
80% to 70%	• A well-developed, systematic, tested, and refined approach in **most** areas, addressing **most** dimensions of the category • A fact-based assessment and improvement process throughout **most** of the organization with few significant gaps • Recognized as an innovative leader in the category • Clear evidence of effectiveness, innovation, and ongoing improvement throughout **most** areas of the organization and its culture
60% to 50%	• An effective, systematic approach, responsive to **many** dimensions of the category • Approach well implemented in **many** areas, although there may be unevenness and inconsistency in particular work groups • A fact-based, systematic process in place for evaluating and improving effectiveness and efficiency in **many** areas • Clear evidence of excellence, innovation, and continuous improvement in **many** areas of the organization and its culture

Percentage Rating Guide

Rating	Approach and Implementation
40% to 30%	• An effective, systematic approach, responsive to **some** dimensions of the category • Approach implemented in **some** areas, but some work areas in the early stages of implementation • A systematic approach to assessing and improving effectiveness and efficiency in **some** areas • Evidence of effectiveness, innovation, and ongoing improvement in **some** areas of the organization and its culture
20% to 10%	• The beginning of a systematic approach to **a few** dimensions of the category • Category criteria addressed in **a few** programs, services, activities, and processes • Major implementation gaps that inhibit progress in achieving the basic purpose of the category • Evidence of effectiveness, innovation, and ongoing improvement in **a few** areas of the organization and its culture
0%	• **No** systematic approach to category, anecdotal information on approach and implementation; not part of the culture of the organization

Percentage Rating Guide Summary

Rating	Approach and Implementation in
90% – 100%	ALL
70% – 80%	MOST
50% – 60%	MANY
30% – 40%	SOME
10% – 20%	A FEW
0%	NO systematic approach or implementation; not part of culture

- Areas, programs, services
- Parts of the culture
- Beneficiary and constituency groups

Your Profile: Note Average Rating for Category 2 and Create a Bar Chart

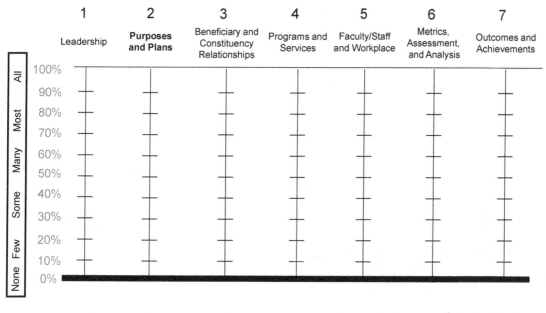

1	2	3	4	5	6	7
Leadership	**Purposes and Plans**	Beneficiary and Constituency Relationships	Programs and Services	Faculty/Staff and Workplace	Metrics, Assessment, and Analysis	Outcomes and Achievements

Category 3: Beneficiary and Constituency Relationships: Focusing on the Groups That Are Important to Your Work

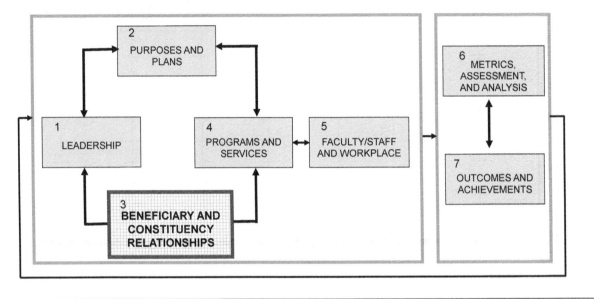

Category 3: Beneficiary and Constituency Relationships

This category focuses on the individuals and groups inside and outside the organization that benefit from the organization's programs and services or with which the organization collaborates, the needs and satisfaction and dissatisfaction of those individuals and groups, and the approaches to gathering and using this information to meet needs and enhance relationships and the organization's reputation.

- Is there a shared view of the relative priority of the groups inside and outside the organization for which the program, department, or institution provides its programs and services?
- Is there a systematic approach to monitoring needs, expectations, satisfaction levels, and the unit's reputation with each group?
- Is information about needs, expectations, satisfaction levels, and perceptions systematically gathered, well organized, analyzed, disseminated, and used for improvement or change? How is this done?
- Are mechanisms in place to ensure effective communication with members of each group?
- Is there a broad commitment to enhancing communication and improving relationships with the groups that are critical to the fulfillment of the mission, aspirations, and goals?

Category 3 Exercise

- What individuals and groups—both inside and outside
  your organization—benefit most from your programs or services?
  Are some more important than others?

- Which of these groups are most central to the fulfillment of your mission,
  aspirations, and goals?

- What methods do you use for facilitating two-way communication,
  assessing needs, and improving relationships with these groups?

- How effective are these methods?

_____
_____
_____
_____
_____
_____
_____
_____
_____
_____
_____
_____
_____
_____
_____
_____

Key Beneficiaries and Constituencies

How are relationships with key groups maintained?

Beneficiary and Constituency Group	Centrality to Missions, Aspirations, and Goals (Rate from 1 to 3) 1 = high 2 = medium 3 = low	Mechanisms for Facilitating Two-way Communication, Assessing Needs, and Improving Relationships	Effectiveness of Mechanisms? (Rate from 1 to 5) 1 = very ineffective 5 = very effective

3: Beneficiary and Constituency Relationships

STRENGTHS	AREAS FOR IMPROVEMENT

_____

_____

_____

_____

_____

_____

_____

_____

_____

_____

_____

_____

_____

_____

_____

_____

_____

_____

Beneficiary and Constituency Relationships

Exemplary Practices

- Genuine commitment to improving the experiences of individuals and groups with whom the organization interacts

- An organization-wide service ethic with a commitment to effectiveness, professionalism, courtesy, and responsiveness visible throughout the organization

- Systematic approaches in place to learn about the needs, expectations, perceptions, and satisfaction and dissatisfaction levels of all stakeholder groups

- Information about beneficiary and constituency needs, expectations, and perceptions disseminated throughout the organization and used to guide planning, day-to-day decision making, and change and improvement

- Emphasis on "frontline" people-to-people encounters, enhancing communication, and building the organization's reputation with campus and external groups

- Strategies in place for anticipating and addressing emerging and predicted needs of stakeholders

- Suggestions and complaints viewed as opportunities, not problems

- Organization widely recognized as a standard setter in building and maintaining strong relationships with beneficiary and constituency groups

Percentage Rating Guide Summary

Rating	Approach and Implementation in
90% – 100%	ALL
70% – 80%	MOST
50% – 60%	MANY
30% – 40%	SOME
10% – 20%	A FEW
0%	NO systematic approach or implementation; not part of culture

- Areas, programs, services
- Parts of the culture
- Beneficiary and constituency groups

Your Profile: Category 3

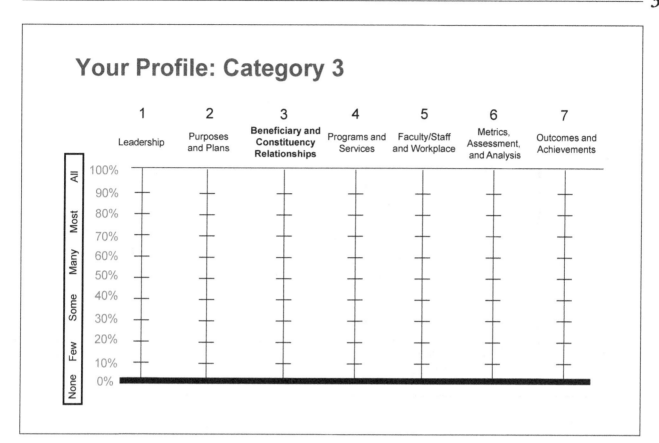

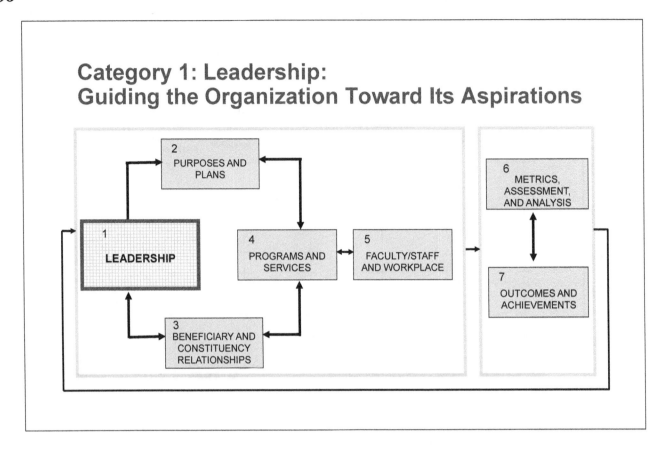

Category 1: Leadership:
Guiding the Organization Toward Its Aspirations

Category 1: Leadership

This category focuses on leadership and governance approaches, how leaders and leadership practices encourage excellence and innovation, and how leadership practices are reviewed and improved.

- Is the leadership and governance structure clearly defined and understood by all?
- How do leadership practices and structures effectively advance the organization's mission and aspirations and promote follow-through on plans and goals?
- Are clearly defined leadership goals in place?
- Do leaders and leadership practices promote active engagement in assessment, planning, and change and improvement by faculty and staff at all levels?
- Are leaders actively engaged with campus, community, and professional or disciplinary groups?
- Are formal and informal leadership review and feedback methods in place and used effectively?
- Is leadership development a core value?

Defining *Leadership*

When we talk about "the leadership,"
we mean . . .

Leadership

Exemplary Practices

- Communicating, clarifying, and helping refine the organization's purposes and plans actively pursued
- Leadership and leadership development encouraged at all levels
- Role modeling evident through personal involvement, collaboration, inspiration, and energy
- High standards of personal ethics and integrity maintained; processes in place to ensure that these values permeate the organization
- Organization's capabilities and aspirations recognized
- Effective communication consistently practiced
- Expressing differing perspectives, thoughtfully listening, and effectively addressing conflict are norms
- Shared understanding and a sense of community actively pursued by leadership
- Ambitious improvement goals established, enthusiasm for change and innovation created, and follow-through ensured
- Dedication to the well-being of the organization, its employees, and the community evident in leadership
- Serving as effective advocates for the organization with external groups
- Procedures in place for developing leadership goals and for using these goals as the basis for systematically reviewing the effectiveness of leadership practices and governance systems
- Feedback on leadership performance encouraged and valued
- Leadership shares expertise outside of the organization and encourages others to do so

Leadership Challenges: A Strength or Area for Improvement?

Leadership Challenge	Strength	Area for Improvement

_____
_____
_____
_____
_____
_____
_____
_____
_____
_____
_____
_____
_____
_____
_____
_____

1: Leadership

STRENGTHS	AREAS FOR IMPROVEMENT

_____
_____
_____
_____
_____
_____
_____
_____
_____
_____
_____
_____
_____
_____

Percentage Rating Guide Summary

Rating	Approach and Implementation in
90% – 100%	ALL
70% – 80%	MOST
50% – 60%	MANY
30% – 40%	SOME
10% – 20%	A FEW
0%	NO systematic approach or implementation; not part of culture

• Areas, programs, services
• Parts of the culture
• Beneficiary and constituency groups

Your Profile: Category 1

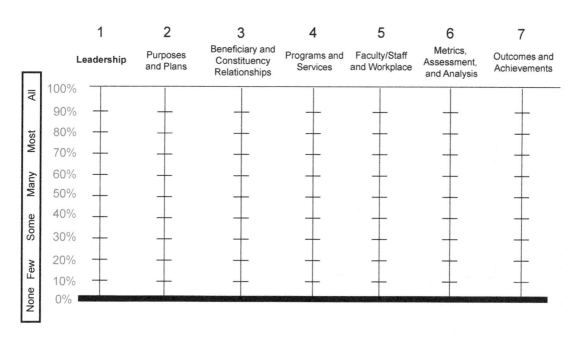

Category 4: Programs and Services: The Essential Work You Do

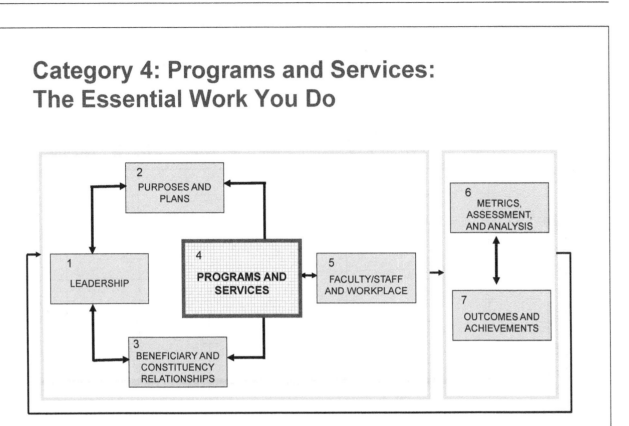

Category 4: Programs and Services

This category focuses on methods for ensuring high standards in mission-critical programs and services and in essential operational and support functions.

- Is there clarity and consensus as to the mission-critical functions of the organization—why the organization exists, what the organization does, and how these functions fit with the mission and aspirations of the institution as a whole?
- Are procedures in place for regular review of programs and services to ensure their quality, continuing relevance, currency, and alignment with the organization's mission and aspirations and those of the institution?
- How do reviews take account of the potential need to refine, revise, or eliminate particular offerings or to create new programs and services?
- What procedures are in place to ensure high standards in the design and implementation of new programs and services and their associated processes?
- Are the key processes associated with mission-critical functions and essential operational and support functions well documented and consistently followed?

A Program or Service Can Be Likened to a Puzzle

- To create the desired outcome, each piece of the puzzle must be thoughtfully and carefully designed and must fit well with other puzzle pieces.
- *Processes* are the puzzle pieces on which the outcomes of programs and services depend.

_____
_____
_____
_____
_____
_____
_____
_____
_____
_____
_____
_____
_____
_____
_____
_____
_____
_____
_____

The Devil–and Often the Key to Excellent Programs and Services–Is in the Details

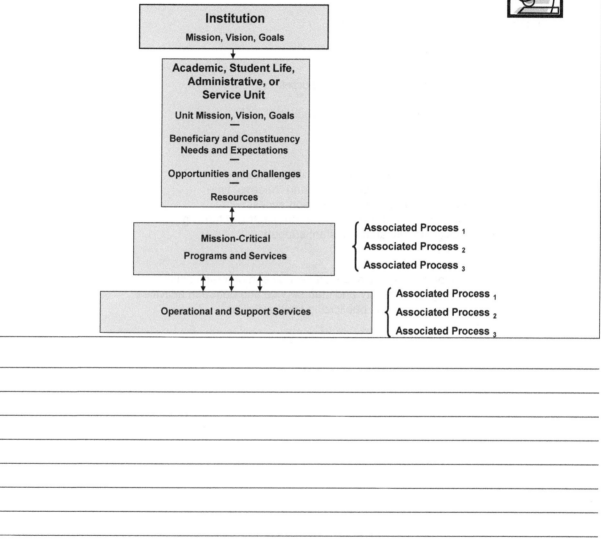

Examples of *Associated Processes* for Mission-Critical Programs and Services

In the case of an **academic unit:**

- Instruction and Teaching
  - Registering
  - Advising
  - Developing and reviewing courses
  - Delivering
  - Evaluating courses and instruction
  - Others
- Scholarship and Research
  - Supporting research services
  - Providing IT research and facility support
  - Providing sabbatical, grants, and "release" time
  - Providing library and information access
  - Generating and allocating conference travel funding
  - Assigning research assistant support
  - Others
- Service and Outreach
  - Supporting faculty and staff service and outreach activities
  - Recognizing faculty and staff service and outreach activities
  - Documenting and publicizing such activities
  - Others

Examples of Operational and Support Service Processes

Operational and Support Processes

Sequences of administrative activities (often "behind the scenes") that are necessary to the fulfillment of the mission

- Recruiting, hiring, retaining
- Administration and clerical support
- Finances and budgeting
- Facilities maintenance
- Purchasing
- IT

Analyzing Processes

Two Examples

An Academic Process Documentation Explains Why It Could Take So Long to Develop a New Course

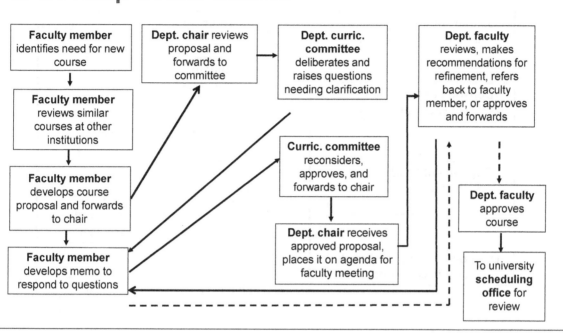

| **Faculty member** identifies need for new course |
| **Faculty member** reviews similar courses at other institutions |
| **Faculty member** develops course proposal and forwards to chair |
| **Faculty member** develops memo to respond to questions |

| **Dept. chair** reviews proposal and forwards to committee |
| **Dept. curric. committee** deliberates and raises questions needing clarification |
| **Dept. faculty** reviews, makes recommendations for refinement, refers back to faculty member, or approves and forwards |

| **Curric. committee** reconsiders, approves, and forwards to chair |
| **Dept. chair** receives approved proposal, places it on agenda for faculty meeting |

| **Dept. faculty** approves course |
| To university **scheduling office** for review |

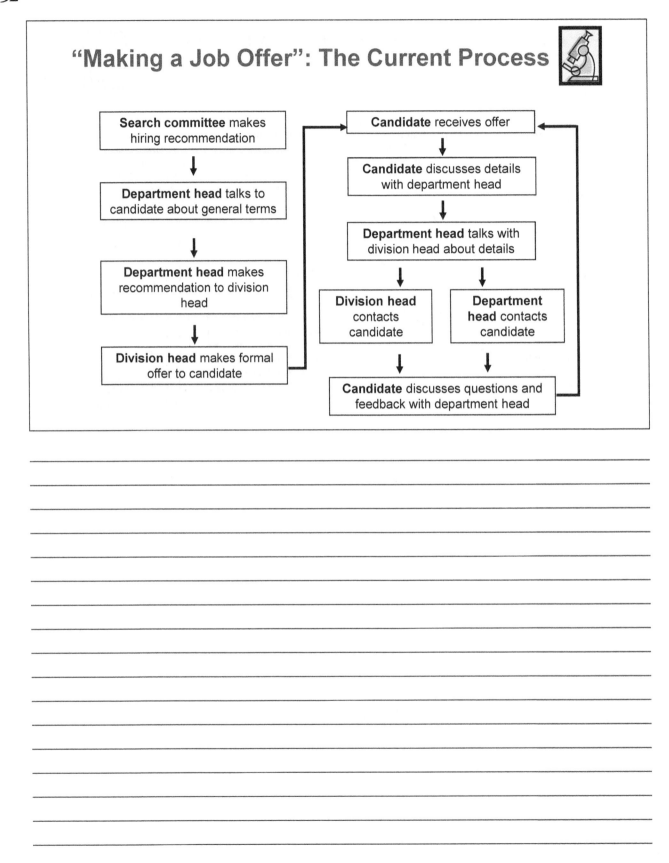

"Making a Job Offer": The Current Process

Search committee makes hiring recommendation

↓

Department head talks to candidate about general terms

↓

Department head makes recommendation to division head

↓

Division head makes formal offer to candidate

Candidate receives offer

↓

Candidate discusses details with department head

↓

Department head talks with division head about details

↓

Division head contacts candidate

Department head contacts candidate

↓

Candidate discusses questions and feedback with department head

"Making a Job Offer": A Revised Process

> **Search committee** makes hiring recommendation

↓

> **Department head** talks with division head about general terms for hiring

↓

> **Department head** talks to candidate about general terms

↓

> **Department head** makes formal offer to candidate

↓

> **Candidate** accepts or declines offer and discusses with department head

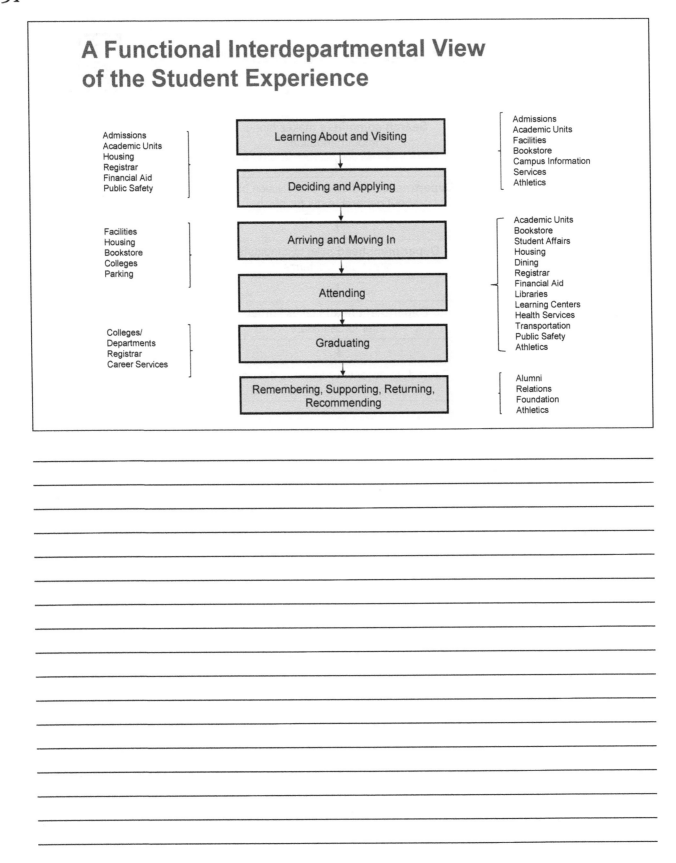

Category 4 Exercise

- What processes are most important to achieving and maintaining the desired outcomes in your mission-critical areas?

- Are these processes designed, standardized, and documented?

- Are these processes regularly reviewed and refined?

Mission-Critical Programs and Services and Associated Processes Matrix

Mission-Critical Programs and Services* (List)	Associated Processes (List)	Standardized (Y/N)	Documented (Y/N)	Regularly Reviewed (Y/N)

* Processes that are essential to the organization's mission and vision.

Mission-Critical Programs and Services and Associated Processes Matrix: An Academic Example

Mission-Critical Programs and Services* (List)	Associated Processes (List)	Standardized (Y/N)	Documented (Y/N)	Regularly Reviewed (Y/N)
Instruction/Teaching (major requirements)	Defining Learning Goals	Y	Y	N
	Scheduling and Assigning Courses	Y	N	N
	Assessing Learning Outcomes	Y	Y	N

* Processes that are essential to the organization's missions and values.

Operational and Support Services Processes Matrix

Operational/Support Programs and Services* (List)	Associated Processes (List)	Standardized (Y/N)	Documented (Y/N)	Regularly Reviewed (Y/N)

* Processes that are essential in support of the mission-critical programs and services.

Operational and Support Services Processess Matrix: An Example

Operational/Support Programs and Services* (List)	Associated Processes (List)	Standardized (Y/N)	Documented (Y/N)	Regularly Reviewed (Y/N)
Information Technology	Establishing Equipment Standards	Y	Y	N
	Ordering Equipment	Y	N	N
	Upgrading Software	Y	N	Y
	Maintaining Equipment	Y	Y	N

* Processes that are essential to the organization's mission.

4: Programs and Services

STRENGTHS	AREAS FOR IMPROVEMENT

Programs and Services

Exemplary Practices

- Clarity as to what programs, services, and activities are critical to the organization's mission
- Alignment between programs and services and the organization's and institution's mission
- Procedures in place to ensure the organization meets high standards on all mission-critical programs and services
- Attention to consistency, assessment, documentation, continuous improvement, and innovation in all programs, services, and processes
- Processes standardized and clear—eliminating the "you just need to know the right person" syndrome
- Attention to detail standard practice in the design, testing, and implementation of key processes
- Effective and efficient operations and support functions a priority, regularly reviewed and improved
- Technological and process innovations are organization-wide values
- Cross-functional groups evaluate and improve processes, requiring collaboration across programs, departments, or institutions
- Comparisons with peers, aspirants, and leaders guide program and service development, implementation, and evaluation
- Programs, services, and processes systematically reviewed on a regular basis and improved, revised, or eliminated based on these reviews

_____

_____

_____

_____

_____

_____

_____

_____

_____

_____

_____

_____

_____

_____

_____

_____

_____

Percentage Rating Guide Summary

Rating	Approach and Implementation in
90% – 100%	ALL
70% – 80%	MOST
50% – 60%	MANY
30% – 40%	SOME
10% – 20%	A FEW
0%	NO systematic approach or implementation; not part of culture

- Areas, programs, services
- Parts of the culture
- Beneficiary and constituency groups

Your Profile: Category 4

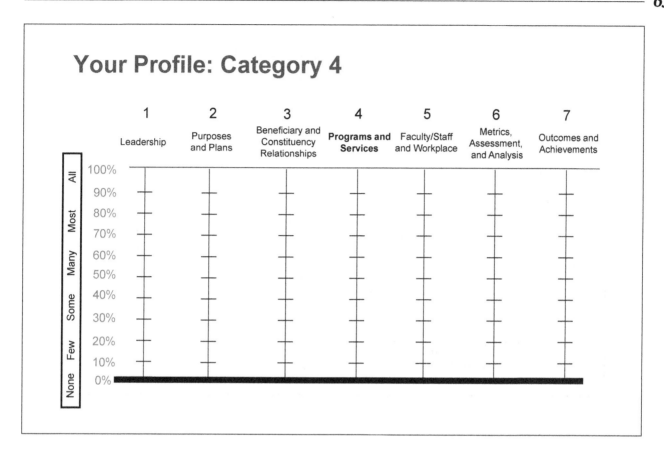

	1	2	3	4	5	6	7
	Leadership	Purposes and Plans	Beneficiary and Constituency Relationships	**Programs and Services**	Faculty/Staff and Workplace	Metrics, Assessment, and Analysis	Outcomes and Achievements

Category 5: Faculty/Staff and Workplace: Attracting and Developing Faculty and Staff: Creating and Maintaining Your Work Environment

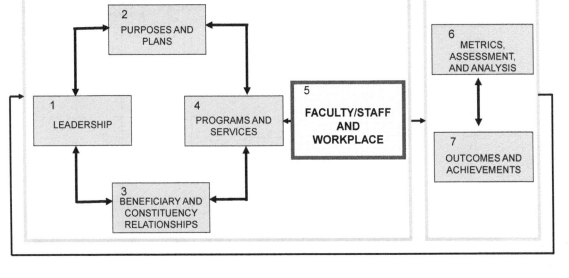

_____
_____
_____
_____
_____
_____
_____
_____
_____
_____
_____
_____
_____
_____
_____
_____
_____
_____
_____

Category 5: Faculty/Staff and Workplace

This category focuses on recruiting and retaining excellent faculty and staff, encouraging and recognizing high standards of performance, promoting professional development, and creating and maintaining effective organizational structures and a positive workplace culture and climate.

- Are faculty and staff qualifications well defined and expectations clear?
- Are systematic and effective procedures in place for identifying, recruiting, hiring, welcoming, and orienting new faculty and staff?
- Are effective approaches in place for encouraging, documenting, and recognizing faculty and staff individual and collaborative accomplishments consistent with the mission, aspirations, and values of the program, department, or institution?
- In what ways are personal and professional development promoted and facilitated?
- Are procedures in place for the regular review and assessment of the effectiveness and efficiency of organizational structures?
- Is there a formalized approach for regularly assessing workplace climate and faculty and staff satisfaction?
- Are procedures in place for the regular assessment of faculty and staff performance?

What Faculty and/or Staff Groups Are Being Considered in This Review?

What faculty and/or staff groups are a part of your organization?

- Tenured and untenured?
- Professional and support?
- Full-time and part-time?
- Unionized and nonunionized?
- Others?

Are all of these groups a focus of this review?

If not, which have you excluded, and why?

_____
_____
_____
_____
_____
_____
_____
_____
_____
_____
_____
_____
_____
_____
_____
_____
_____
_____

Faculty/Staff and Workplace

Exemplary Practices
- High standards of individual performance and collaborative accomplishment recognized and rewarded as organization-wide values
- Meaningful review, reward, and recognition programs link individual and group accomplishments to the directions, aspirations, and priorities of the organization
- Translating stated values and principles into practice recognized and rewarded within the organization
- Available programs include welcome and orientation programs, career progression planning, and job enrichment opportunities for all employee groups
- Innovation and continuous improvement are organization-wide values
- Systematic programs assess workplace climate and faculty and staff satisfaction, with procedures in place to address identified improvement needs
- A shared sense of pride in the organization and a general feeling that "this is a great place to work"
- A general feeling that "my opinion counts"
- Professional development emphasized in principle and in practice

5: Faculty/Staff and Workplace

STRENGTHS	AREAS FOR IMPROVEMENT

Percentage Rating Guide Summary

Rating	Approach and Implementation in
90% – 100%	ALL
70% – 80%	MOST
50% – 60%	MANY
30% – 40%	SOME
10% – 20%	A FEW
0%	NO systematic approach or implementation; not part of culture

- Areas, programs, services
- Parts of the culture
- Beneficiary and constituency groups

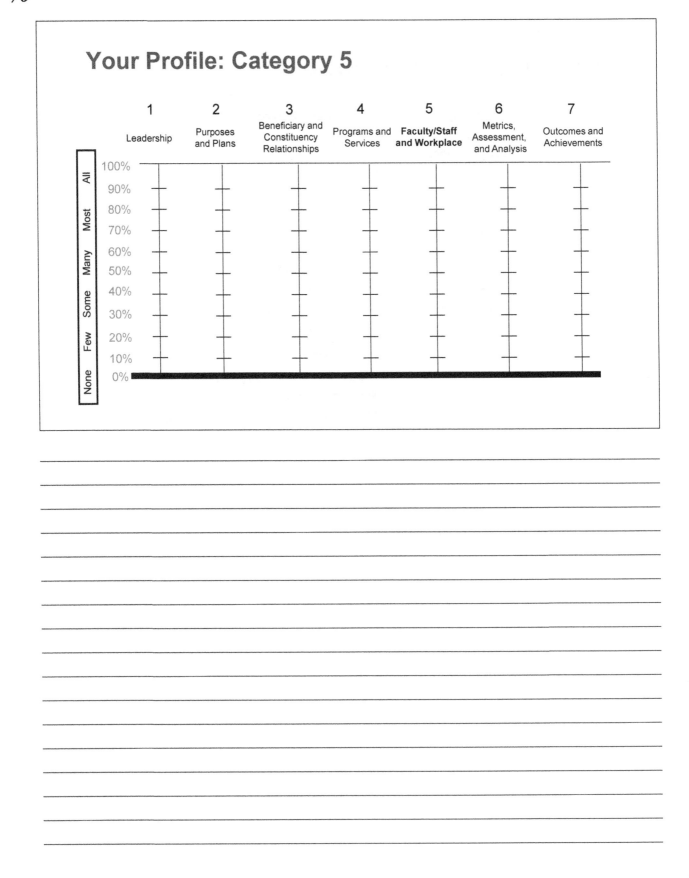

Your Profile: Category 5

| | 1
Leadership | 2
Purposes and Plans | 3
Beneficiary and Constituency Relationships | 4
Programs and Services | 5
Faculty/Staff and Workplace | 6
Metrics, Assessment, and Analysis | 7
Outcomes and Achievements |

Category 6: Metrics, Assessment, and Analysis: Deciding How to Measure Effectiveness and Quality

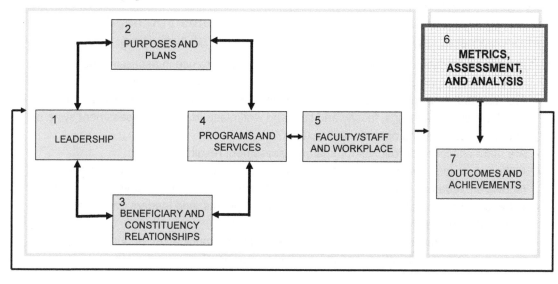

Category 6: Metrics, Assessment, and Analysis

This category considers the metrics and methods used for review and analysis of the effectiveness of the institution, department, or program. It focuses on how assessment metrics are developed and used to identify and document accomplishments and needs for the improvement, innovation, or discontinuation of activities.

- Is there a well-defined, shared view as to what standards to use in assessing the effectiveness of the organization in achieving its mission and aspirations?
- Are standards in place for assessing leadership practices, planning, beneficiary and constituency relationships, faculty and staff and workplace functions, assessment systems, and administrative and operational functions?
- Are there effective approaches for sharing assessment results?
- Is this information effectively used to guide organizational improvement: refinement, innovation, redesign, and the discontinuation of particular programs, services, or activities?
- Is trend and comparative information from peers, aspirants, and leaders gathered, analyzed, and used to evaluate, improve, and innovate?
- Is outcome information used in internal and external communication, priority setting, planning, resource allocation, and reward and recognition?

Assessment: The 30,000-Foot View: "Mission-to-Measures"

Activity / Project / Organization

Mission, Vision, Values, Priorities

- Leadership
- Purposes and Plans
- Beneficiary and Constituency Relationships
- Programs and Services
- Faculty/Staff and Workplace
- Metrics, Assessment, and Analysis

Measures

What is our focus? ⟹ How will we know if we're successful?

Steps to Develop an Integrated Assessment Process

1. Define or Clarify Goals
- Identify and consider the needs and expectations of beneficiaries and constituencies and other key factors.
- Establish clear and shared goals for program and service areas and offerings.
- Be certain that goals cover the full range of relevant activities.
- Clearly communicate goals to beneficiaries and constituencies.

2. Evaluate Outcomes
- Use established goals to guide assessment activities at all levels in your institution, department, or program.
- Develop and use appropriate outcome indicators, criteria, measures, and evaluative procedures.
- Assess the extent to which established goals are being met within program and service areas and more generally and identify gaps.
- Assess progress by examining patterns and trends.
- Make comparisons with peers, aspirants, and leaders at other institutions.
- Confirm that assessment covers all defined goals and other factors associated with institutional effectiveness.

3. Use the Assessment Outcome Information
- Communicate the results of assessment to colleagues within the institution and to beneficiary and constituency groups, as appropriate.
- Compare outcome information, as appropriate, with results from previous years and with those from peer, aspirant, and leading organizations to identify improvement targets.
- Use outcome information to improve programs and services and the effectiveness of the institution, department, or program more generally.
- Integrate outcome information into formal and informal planning and decision-making activities.
- Periodically review and, as appropriate, refine and update your goals, assessment procedures, and approaches to using this information.

_____

_____

_____

_____

_____

_____

_____

_____

_____

_____

_____

_____

_____

_____

_____

_____

_____

_____

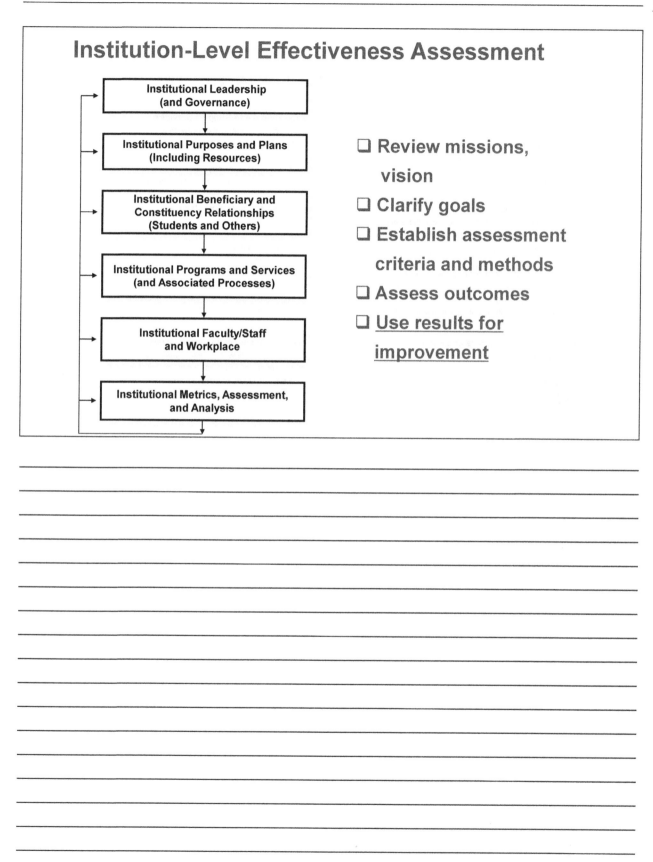

Institution-Level Effectiveness Assessment

Institutional Leadership (and Governance)

Institutional Purposes and Plans (Including Resources)

Institutional Beneficiary and Constituency Relationships (Students and Others)

Institutional Programs and Services (and Associated Processes)

Institutional Faculty/Staff and Workplace

Institutional Metrics, Assessment, and Analysis

❑ Review missions, vision
❑ Clarify goals
❑ Establish assessment criteria and methods
❑ Assess outcomes
❑ Use results for improvement

Potential Assessment Indicators for Administrative and Service Departments

Leadership
- Effectiveness ratings by colleagues and peers
- Performance review results
- Progress on leadership priorities and projects
- Contributions to campus, community, and professional organizations

Purposes and Plans
- Progress on review of mission and vision realization
- Progress in establishing a formalized strategic planning process
- Progress on plans and goals

Beneficiary and Constituency Relationships
- Satisfaction ratings
- Satisfaction with programs and services
- Positive and improving reputation for quality and service

Mission-Critical Programs and Services
- Effectiveness
- Efficiency
- Reliability
- Cycle time
- Resource utilization

Operational and Support Services
- Financial management effectiveness
- Staff recruiting and training effectiveness
- Policy and regulation adherence
- Adequacy of technology
- Effectiveness and efficiency of equipment

Faculty/Staff and Workplace
- Recruitment
- Attractiveness
- Turnover and retention
- Compensation
- Organizational culture and climate
- Morale
- Professional courses and programs offered and taken
- Recognition provided

Metrics, Assessment, and Analysis
- Rating of progress in developing assessment system
- Implementation of new assessment tools and methods
- Dissemination of assessment results
- Use of outcomes information for improvement

Indicators of Learning

Direct Indicators of Learning

- Entrance pretests and exit (or post-) tests (course specific and program specific)
- Placement tests
- Portfolio assessment (multiple reviewers)
- Capstone experiences (e.g., course, thesis, field project)
- Respected standardized tests and internally and externally designed comprehensive (written and oral) exit tests and examinations
- Senior thesis (multiple reviewers)
- Oral defense of senior thesis or project (multiple reviewers)
- Required oral presentations (multiple raters)
- National tests and examinations
- Performance on licensure, certification, or professional exams
- Essay questions (blind cored by multiple faculty)
- Required papers and research projects (multiple reviewers)
- Internal and external juried review of comprehensive senior projects
- Externally reviewed exhibits and performances
- External evaluation of internship performance

Indirect Indicators of Learning

- Exit interviews of graduates and focus groups
- Surveys of alumni, employers, and students
- Retention, persistence, graduation, and transfer rates and studies
- Length of time to degree (years or hours to completion)
- Grade distributions
- SAT scores
- Course enrollments and profiles
- Job placement data

Other Indicators of Learning

- Questionnaires asking students if their personal goals for course, major, or program have been met
- Instruments that collect data on indirect facts that can affect student success such as curriculum review reportsor evaluation reports of program submitted by visiting committees of external peer experts (accreditation reports)
- Faculty publications and recognition
- Courses selected by majors, grades, and GPAs
- Percentage of students who study abroad
- Enrollment trends
- Student diversity

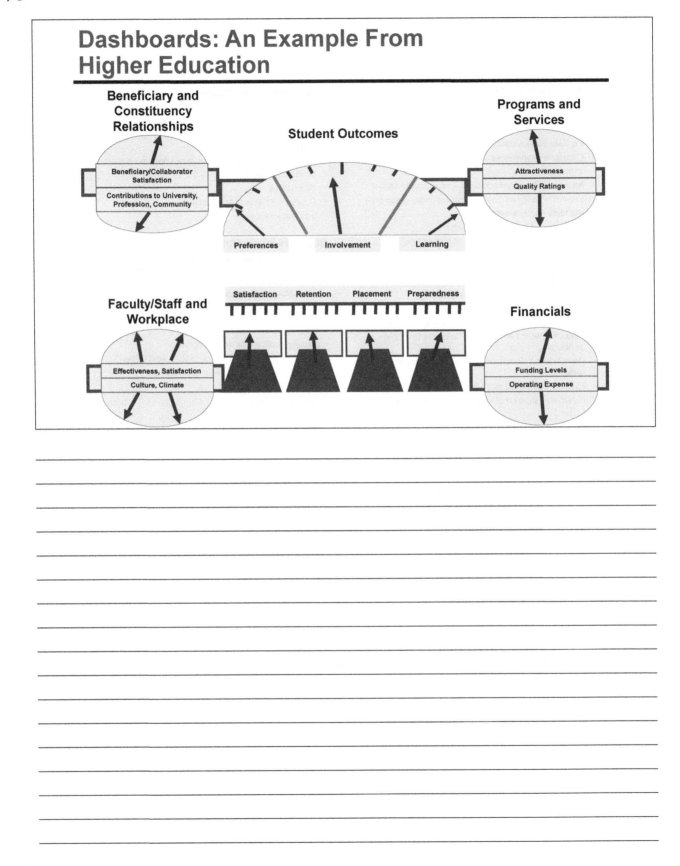

Dashboards: An Example From Higher Education

Benefits of Metrics, Assessment, and Analysis

- Stimulates dialogue and clarifies the organization's mission, aspirations, values, and priorities
- Heightens shared sense of the purposes of programs and services
- Develops shared perspective on standards and indicators of excellence
- Identifies current strengths
- Clarifies and provides information on change, innovation, and improvement needs
- Provides meaningful comparisons
- Heightens personal and collective responsibility
- Encourages, monitors, and documents progress
- Provides foundation for fact-based planning, decision making, and problem solving
- Energizes and motivates

Category 6 Exercise: Measures Matrix (example)

Area/Category	Current Measures	Source of Information	Compare Outcomes	Outcomes Use
1: Leadership	Effectiveness ratings, external or campus contributions, rate of success of hiring and promotion, unit prominence and visibility	Surveys, review of reports, media coverage	Compare to other units	Use in planning, workplace climate assessment
2: Purposes and Plans	Progress on plans, goals achieved, and extent of faculty and staff participation in planning	Review strategic planning records, participation rates	Compare to last year	Input to plan assessment
3: Beneficiary and Constituency Relationships	Reputation, perceptions of stakeholders, scope of stakeholder focus, complaints	Surveys, focus groups, review of suggestions and complaint reports	Compare to last year and peers	Change or improvements to communication and organizational practices
4: Programs and Services	Usage, satisfaction	Internal records, participant surveys	Streamline procedures, revise procedures	Compare to last year
5: Faculty/Staff and Workplace	Qualifications, recruitment success, record of achievements, retention, satisfaction	Review of internal records, staff surveys	Compare to last year and peers, aspirants	Develop formal recognition programs
6: Metrics, Assessment, and Analysis	Extent and functionality of assessment system in place, documented use of information	Review of internal records	Compare to last year and peers, aspirants	Use in planning and change or improvements throughout organization

Category 6 Exercise: Measures Matrix

Area/Category	Current Measures	Source of Information	Compare Outcomes	Outcomes Use
1: Leadership				
2: Purposes and Plans				
3: Beneficiary and Constituency Relationships				
4: Programs and Services				

Category 6 Exercise: Measures Matrix

Area/Category	Current Measures	Source of Information	Compare Outcomes	Outcomes Use
5: Faculty/Staff and Workplace				
6: Metrics, Assessment, and Analysis				

_____

_____

_____

_____

_____

_____

_____

_____

_____

_____

_____

_____

_____

_____

_____

_____

_____

Selected Metrics Should . . .

- Reflect important institution, department, or program strategic priorities and performance dimensions
- Utilize data that will be helpful in identifying accomplishments and also areas in need of revision, innovation, redesign, reinvention, or, if appropriate, discontinuation
- Reflect stakeholder needs
- Be communicable to—and easily understandable by—a broad audience
- Provide the basis for comparisons with other institutions and internal or external departments or programs
- Have a reasonable cost-benefit relationship (cost of obtaining data versus value in having data)
- Utilize data that will be available over a period of years

Metrics, Assessment, and Analysis

Exemplary Practices

- Outcome and achievement indicators anchored in organizational and institutional mission, vision, values, goals, and priorities
- A comprehensive set of indicators in place for assessing organizational effectiveness in all categories and areas
- A systematic portfolio of metrics used in identifying accomplishments and areas in need of innovation, improvement, redesign, or discontinuation
- Systems in place to ensure wide access to—and use of—outcomes and achievements information
- Knowledge, expertise, and effective practices information shared and utilized throughout the organization
- Appropriate peer, aspirant, and leader comparisons identified, and information-gathering and exchange processes in place to allow for comparisons in all categories
- Assessment information tracked over time to identify trends and their implications
- Organizational measures and comparisons used to assess effectiveness, create focus, and guide day-to-day decision making, resource allocation, planning, improvement, and innovation

_____

_____

_____

_____

_____

_____

_____

_____

_____

_____

_____

_____

_____

_____

_____

_____

_____

_____

_____

6: Metrics, Assessment, and Analysis

STRENGTHS	AREAS FOR IMPROVEMENT

_____
_____
_____
_____
_____
_____
_____
_____
_____
_____
_____
_____
_____
_____
_____

Percentage Rating Guide Summary

Rating	Approach and Implementation in
90% – 100%	ALL
70% – 80%	MOST
50% – 60%	MANY
30% – 40%	SOME
10% – 20%	A FEW
0%	NO systematic approach or implementation; not part of culture

- Areas, programs, services
- Parts of the culture
- Beneficiary and constituency groups

Your Profile: Category 6

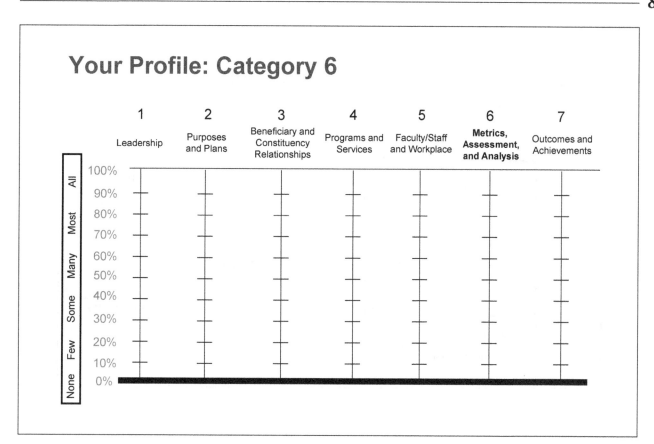

Category 7: Outcomes and Achievements:
What the Results Demonstrate About Effectiveness

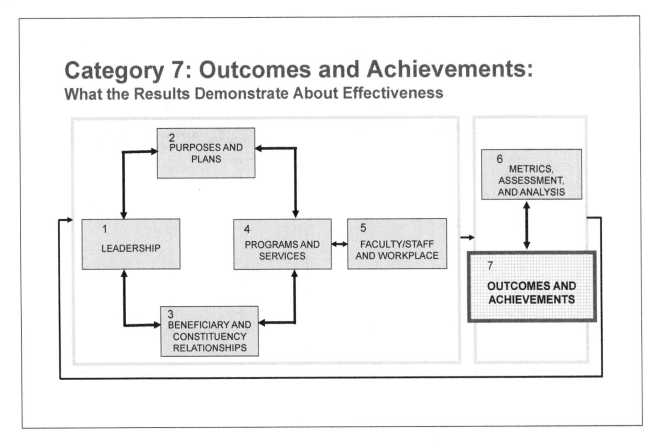

Category 7: Outcomes and Achievements

This category focuses on evidence documenting outcomes, achievements, and impact; progress over time relative to plans and goals; and effectiveness compared to peers, aspirants, and leaders.

- What does objective outcome information indicate about the organization's success in achieving its mission, vision, plans, goals, and priorities?
- What does objective outcome information indicate about the effectiveness of mission-critical programs and services?
- What does the available information indicate about the effectiveness of leadership, planning, beneficiary and constituency relations, faculty/staff and workplace quality and satisfaction, metrics, metrics assessment, and documenting and reporting outcomes?
- How do evidence and information compare to trends with peer, aspirant, and leader outcomes?
- How is outcome information used for continuing improvement and innovation and for communicating with internal and external constituencies?

7: Outcomes and Achievements

STRENGTHS	AREAS FOR IMPROVEMENT

Category 6 and Category 7:
An Analogy: Your Organization's Report Card

Your Report Card

Category 6

- On what should you be graded?

-Reading

-Writing

-Math

-Plays well with others

Category 7

- What grade did you get?
- Are you improving over time?
- How do you compare to others?

A	Y	A
B-	N	B
B	Y	B-
C	N	C-

Category 7: Leadership: An Example

Indicators: What We Currently Measure	Outcomes for This Year (+/-/flat)	Compared to Previous Years (+/-/flat)	Compared to Plans and Goals (+/-/flat)	Compared to Peers and Leaders (+/-/flat)
Results from leadership survey in the areas of:				
Internal communication	+	+	+	?
External communication	-	F	-	?
Effectiveness rating	+	+	+	+
Progress on 2015 leadership initiatives	+	?	+	?
Fund-raising	+	+	+	+
Other				

? = "Don't have information on this" or "Don't know"

Leadership Outcomes

Indicators: What We Currently Measure	Outcomes for This Year (+/-/flat)	Compared to Previous Years (+/-/flat)	Compared to Plans and Goals (+/-/flat)	Compared to Peers and Leaders (+/-/flat)

? = "Don't have information on this" or "Don't know"

Purposes and Plans Outcomes

Indicators: What We Currently Measure	Outcomes for This Year (+/-/flat)	Compared to Previous Years (+/-/flat)	Compared to Plans and Goals (+/-/flat)	Compared to Peers and Leaders (+/-/flat)

? = "Don't have information on this" or "Don't know"

Beneficiary and Constituency Relationships Outcomes

Indicators: What We Currently Measure	Outcomes for This Year (+/-/flat)	Compared to Previous Years (+/-/flat)	Compared to Plans and Goals (+/-/flat)	Compared to Peers and Leaders (+/-/flat)

? = "Don't have information on this" or "Don't know"

Programs and Services Outcomes

Indicators: What We Currently Measure	Outcomes for This Year (+/-/flat)	Compared to Previous Years (+/-/flat)	Compared to Plans and Goals (+/-/flat)	Compared to Peers and Leaders (+/-/flat)

? = "Don't have information on this" or "Don't know"

Faculty/Staff and Workplace Outcomes

Indicators: What We Currently Measure	Outcomes for This Year (+/-/flat)	Compared to Previous Years (+/-/flat)	Compared to Plans and Goals (+/-/flat)	Compared to Peers and Leaders (+/-/flat)

? = "Don't have information on this" or "Don't know"

Metrics, Assessment, and Analysis Outcomes

Indicators: What We Currently Measure	Outcomes for This Year (+/-/flat)	Compared to Previous Years (+/-/flat)	Compared to Plans and Goals (+/-/flat)	Compared to Peers and Leaders (+/-/flat)

? = "Don't have information on this" or "Don't know"

Outcomes and Achievements
Exemplary Practices

- Distinguished institution, department, or program, recognized for excellence locally, regionally, and nationally

- Programs and services—and the organization overall—recognized as among the best of their kind anywhere

- Positive and sustained outcomes and achievements documented in the areas of leadership, purposes and plans, beneficiary and constituency relationships, programs and services, faculty/staff satisfaction and workplace climate, metrics and assessment, and in terms of fulfilling the overall mission, vision, and broad organizational goals

- No unfavorable outcomes or trends in key categories or areas

- Record of significant achievement, innovation, and continuing improvement in effectiveness, productivity, value, and efficiency, particularly in mission-critical processes

- Favorable comparison outcomes documented in all of these areas in relation to peer, aspirant, and leading organizations

Category 7 Percentage Rating Guide Summary: Focus on Outcomes

Rating	Outcomes and Achievements in
90% – 100%	ALL
70% – 80%	MOST
50% – 60%	MANY
30% – 40%	SOME
10% – 20%	A FEW
0%	NO systematic approach or implementation; not part of culture

- Documented results
- Positive outcomes and trends
- Comparisons provided
- Positive comparative outcomes

Your Profile: Category 7

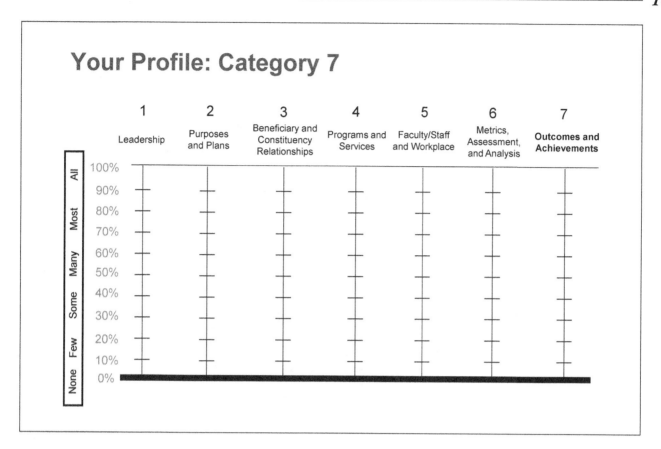

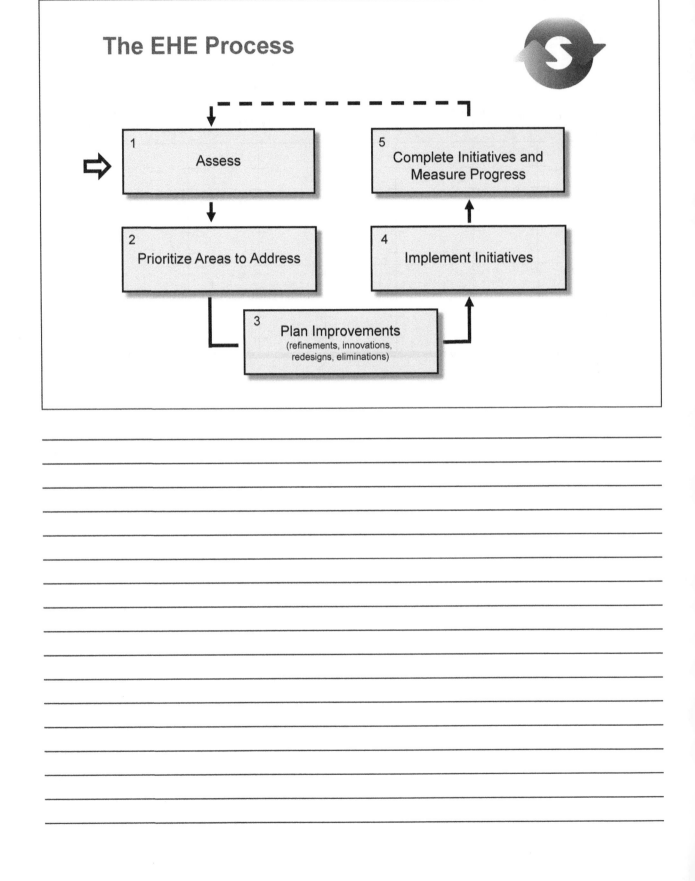

Excellence in Higher Education:
The Framework and Categories

Dimensions for Program, Departmental, or Institutional Effectiveness

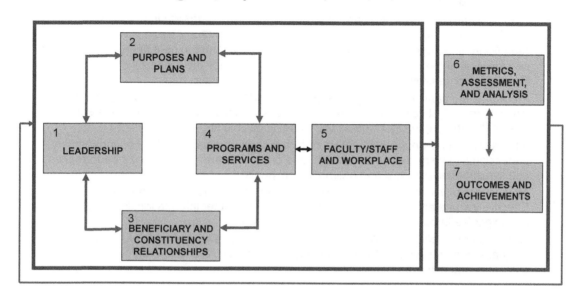

EHE Themes

- *Leadership.* Define, communicate, and model a commitment to the purposes, plans, and people of the organization.
- *Purposes and plans.* Set clear directions and aspirations, translate into plans with ambitious goals, and see those plans through to completion.
- *Beneficiary and constituency relationships.* Listen to and understand the needs and perspectives of the groups served and those that influence the organization's work. Develop an organization-wide service ethic. Identify and close gaps.
- *Programs and services.* Identify, analyze, standardize, and continuously improve and innovate the effectiveness of programs, services, and their associated processes to ensure that the organization meets the highest possible standards.
- *Faculty/staff and workplace.* Create a culture that encourages excellence, engagement, professional development, commitment, and pride. Reward and recognize performance and synchronize individual and organizational goals.
- *Metrics, assessment, and analysis.* Assess quality and effectiveness in all areas. Effectively share and use the assessment results and other information, knowledge, and expertise throughout the organization and beyond.
- *Outcomes and achievements.* Document progress, achievements, and outcomes and compare these results with those of peers, aspirants, and leaders. Communicate outcomes and achievements widely.

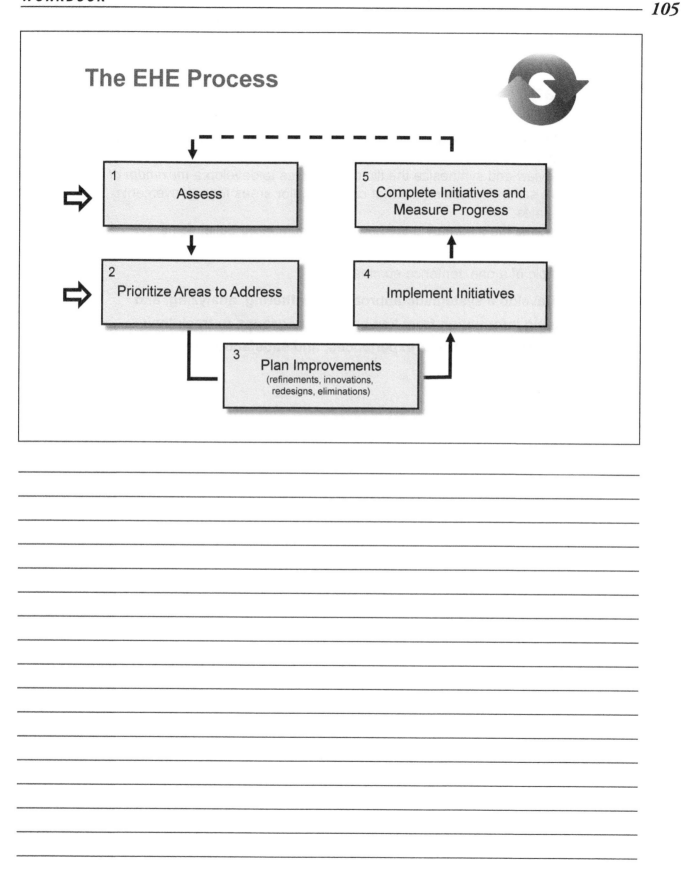

The EHE Process

1 Assess

2 Prioritize Areas to Address

3 Plan Improvements
(refinements, innovations, redesigns, eliminations)

4 Implement Initiatives

5 Complete Initiatives and Measure Progress

Summarizing Strengths and Change and Improvement Priorities

- Review the list of identified areas for improvement developed in each category.
- Review and synthesize the flip chart entries to develop a *maximum of five* summary statements that capture major areas for improvement themes.
- Rewrite the summary statements as unnumbered bullet items.

Example of a one-sentence summary:

"Develop a systematic approach to gathering, analyzing, and using information from key beneficiary groups to track their needs, expectations, experiences, and satisfaction levels."

_____

_____

_____

_____

_____

_____

_____

_____

_____

_____

_____

_____

_____

_____

_____

_____

_____

Prioritizing Areas to Address

- Post and read through areas for improvement summary statements.
- Provide any needed clarifications and eliminate any duplication.
- Multi-vote to prioritize areas for change or improvement: Each individual indicates the *three* that are the highest priority (by making a pencil or pen mark next to the items).
- Before beginning, review the criteria on the next slide.
- Alternatively, the following slide can be used to prioritize areas for improvement.

Criteria to Consider
When Prioritizing Initiatives

- ✓ Impact

- ✓ Urgency

- ✓ Within your control and capability

- ✓ Prerequisite to a larger initiative

- ✓ Organizational support available

- ✓ Benefits organization as a whole

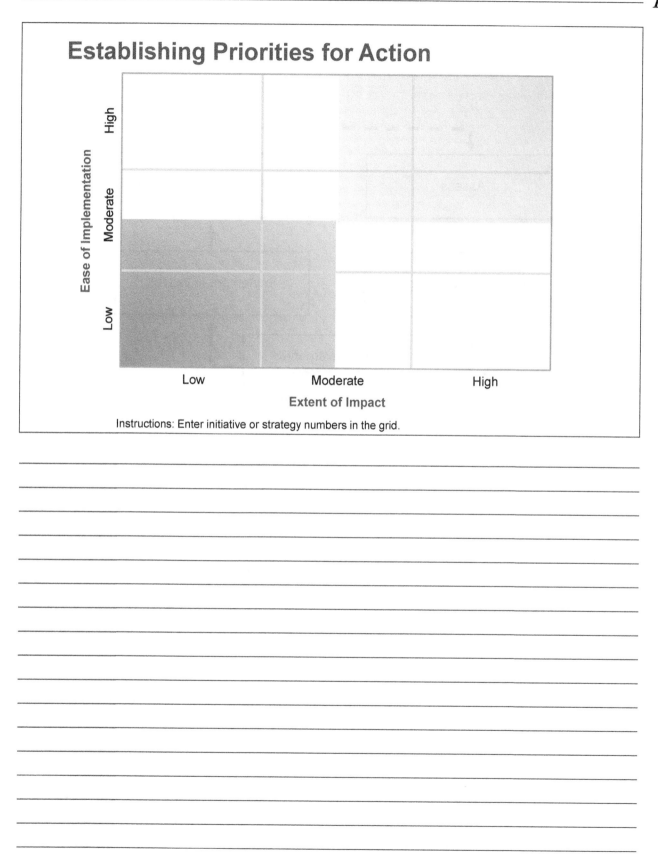

Establishing Priorities for Action

Ease of Implementation
- High
- Moderate
- Low

Extent of Impact
- Low
- Moderate
- High

Instructions: Enter initiative or strategy numbers in the grid.

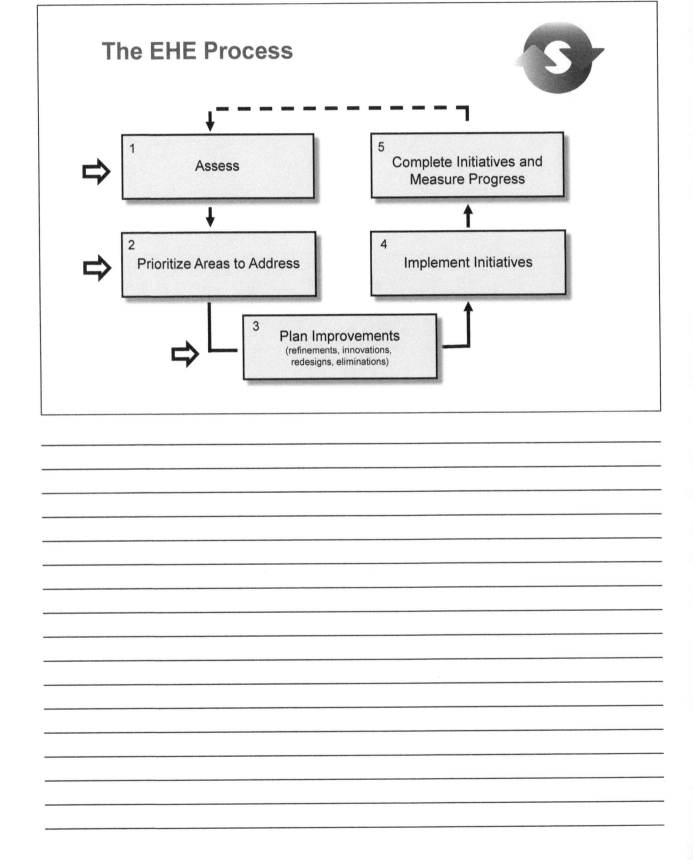

Moving to Action Planning

- Following voting, identify the top-ranked changes and improvements.

- Develop preliminary action plans using the template on the following slide.

*For each change or improvement area the group has selected as a priority, develop a **project action plan** by specifying the following:*

Priority/initiative/goal no. _____

_____ Short term (six months or less)

Project (strategy) description:

_____ Longer term (seven months to one year)

Key steps and activities:

Potential group members:

Convener:

Funding considerations:

Deliverables:

Communication and engagement issues:

Time frame (start-up, milestones, target completion date):

Effectiveness measures:

How to move the project to action (multiple choice):

❑ Delegate to existing group (if so, which one?)
❑ Delegate to individual (if so, whom?)
❑ Delegate to leadership
❑ Form task force

Sample Project Planning Template

Priority/initiative/goal no. _____   ____ Short term (six months or less)

Project (strategy) description: ____ Longer term (seven months to one year)
In one or two sentences, how can you clearly define the scope of the project?

Key steps and activities:
What kinds of broad activities need to be part
of the project plan?

Potential group members:
Which individuals or positions need to be represented in
the group to bring the best input, ideas, and expertise to
the project? Who should chair or lead the group?

Convener:

Funding considerations: What resources are required to make the project a reality? To sustain it?
What sources currently exist? What issues exist?

Deliverables: At the end of the project, what items will the group produce (e.g., a report, a new or revised
process, a survey, a website, publications)?

Communication and engagement issues: How will you keep others abreast of your progress? How will you
promote two-way communication about the project? How will you let others know about recommendations/changes?

Time frame (start-up, milestones, target completion date): What is a reasonable amount of time for the
project? (Keep in mind operational calendar, lead time for notification of changes, etc.)

Effectiveness measures:
What information will tell you whether the planning has been successful in reaching the desired outcomes?

How to move the project to action (multiple choice): What needs to be done to ensure the project moves
❑ Delegate to existing group (if so, which one?)   forward?
❑ Delegate to individual (if so, whom?)
❑ Delegate to leadership
❑ Form task force

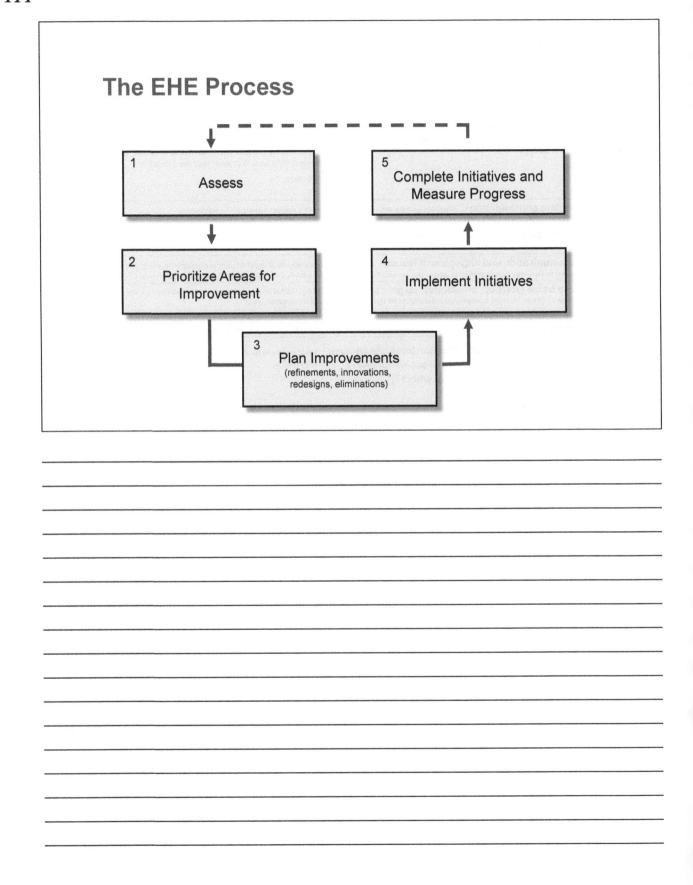

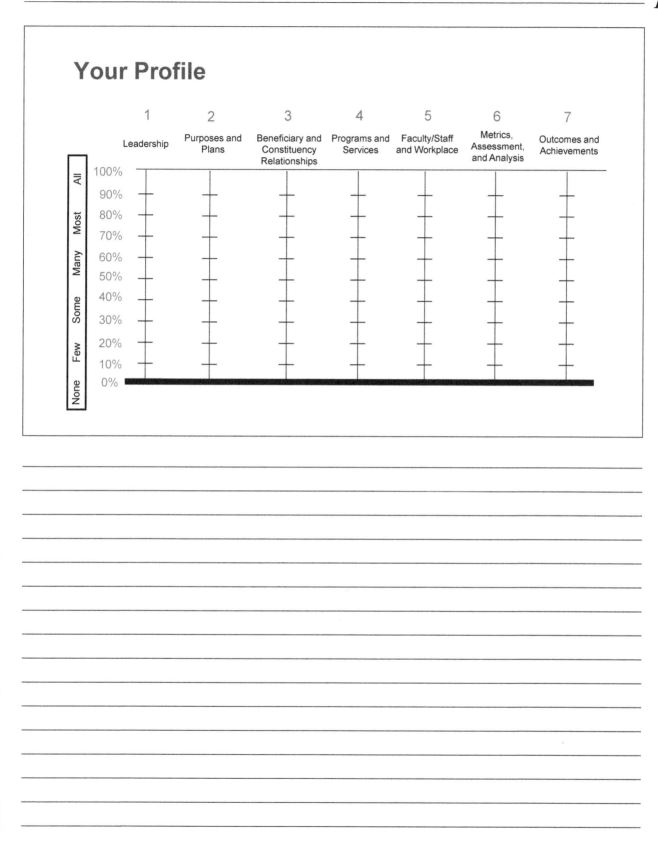

Your Profile

Appendix: Examples of Summary Charts

Sample Summary Chart, Categories 1–6

Table W.1: Summary Analysis of Categories 1–6, Approach and Implementation, for Unit 1					
Categories	Strengths	Areas for Improvement	Good	Acceptable	Needs to Be Addressed
1. Leadership	• Leaders are open to feedback • Visible dedication • Leadership effectiveness feedback system has been developed • Commitment to generating funds • Active external representation by leaders on campus	• Need to increase encouragement of entrepreneurial activity • Increase active external representation by leaders within community and field	X		
2. Purposes and Plans	• Clear, differentiated, and shared sense of purpose and future direction • Several programs within the unit have operational plans • A new planning process is being developed and will be implemented next year	• Address resources as a part of planning process • Need environmental assessment to identify strengths, weaknesses, and particularly threats and opportunities • Need a more formalized planning process	X		
3. Beneficiary and Constituency Relationships	• High-quality access to faculty/staff • Faculty dedicated to students • Staff emphasize service orientation • A number of mechanisms in place for identifying student and workplace needs	• Improve website and other electronic systems for communicating with students • Need more systematic approaches to gathering data on stakeholder needs, experiences, and expectations		X	
4. Programs and Services	• Establishing new advising system • Committee has been formed to review the major requirements • Good laboratory facilities	• Review and update curricula • Improve support and resources for teaching and scholarship • Increase outreach and community engagement		X	
5. Faculty/Staff and Workplace	• Sense of community, especially among senior faculty and staff	• Need to establish mentoring system for young faculty • Improve professional travel support for faculty and staff • Review effectiveness of Organizational structure			X
6. Metrics, Assessment, and Analysis	• Some useful information is available • Some assessment measures and indicators are in place	• Need to systematize gathering, implementation, and use of the assessment in all areas		X	
Composite rating in Approach and Implementation for Unit 1				X	

Developed by Brent D. Ruben and Nagi Naganathan

Sample Summary Chart, Category 7

Categories	Favorable Outcomes	Marginal Outcomes	Good	Acceptable	Needs to Be Addressed
Table W.2: Summary Analysis of Category 7, Outcomes and Achievements, for Unit 1					
1. Leadership Outcomes	• Positive results on internal leadership effectiveness (average rating: 4.2/5.0) • Oversight of successful planning effort (6/7 goals) • 22% increase in funds for unit	• Improved faculty meetings noted as area in need of improvement on survey • External leadership in campus and discipline	X		
2. Purposes and Plans Outcomes	• Significant progress on 6 of 7 goals • Majority of faculty involved in implementation of strategic plan	• Improve progress on 1 of 7 goals including clarification of responsible parties	X		
3. Beneficiary and Constituency Relationships Outcomes	• Evidence of perceived need among students and workplace professionals • Course/instructor evaluations at or above the university average in 65% of courses • Strong evidence of effectiveness of outreach program to prospective students • Alumni survey initiated and results used as basis for improvement and review of curriculum	• Survey results show dissatisfaction with advising • Survey results reveal dissatisfaction with introductory courses	X		
4. Programs and Services Outcomes	• Three new elective courses implemented	• Curricula has not been reviewed within last five years • No systematic process in place for curricula review • Publication and scholarly productivity of faculty does not compare favorably with previous years or with peers (trending downward) • No established teaching/learning goals or outcome measures			X
5. Faculty/Staff and Workplace Outcomes	• Established new faculty mentoring system, rated as very effective by all new faculty	• Three highly regarded faculty left for positions elsewhere • Two unit tenure recommendations were reversed at higher level			X
6. Metrics, Assessment, and Analysis Outcomes	• Assessment measures/indicators were used in design of new courses • Leadership effectiveness feedback system was established and used to provide feedback			X	
Composite rating in Outcomes and Achievements for Unit 1			X		

Developed by Brent D. Ruben and Nagi Naganathan

Sample Summary Chart for Multiple Units

Table W.3: Assessment Results and Recommendations at Division, College, and Institutional Levels		
Level 1 **Recognize, Encourage, Consider Increasing Support**	**Level 2** **Continue, Consider Increasing Support**	**Level 3** **Continue or Discontinue, Consider Decreasing Support**
• Favorable Approach and Implementation • Favorable Outcomes and Achievements **Other Considerations:** • Adequacy of internal resources • Alignment with directions and future plans of division, college, or institution	• Acceptable Approach and Implementation • Acceptable Outcomes and Achievements **Other Considerations:** • Adequacy of internal resources • Alignment with directions and future plans of division, college, or institution	• Marginal Approach and Implementation • Marginal Outcomes and Achievements **Other Considerations:** • Adequacy of internal resources • Alignment with directions and future plans of division, college, or institution
1. Unit 01 2. Unit 03 3. Unit 04	1. Unit 06 2. Unit 07	1. Unit 02 2. Unit 05

Developed by Brent D. Ruben and Nagi Naganathan

The Evaluation and Scoring Process

EACH OF THE SEVEN EHE categories is an important dimension of organizational excellence. For purposes of analysis, the EHE approach "freezes" the ongoing dynamics of an institution, department, or program and focuses on each component individually to clarify organizational strengths and to identify potential areas for improvement. Figure W.1 summarizes the areas addressed within each category.

Approach, Implementation, and Outcomes

Categories 1 through 6 focus on *approach* and *implementation*, whereas Category 7 focuses *outcomes*.

Approach refers to the methods and strategies used by an organization. *Approach* is evaluated based on the extent to which the methods and strategies used are

- ✓ Effective
- ✓ Systematic
- ✓ Integrated
- ✓ Innovative
- ✓ Consistently applied
- ✓ Based on reliable information
- ✓ Regularly evaluated and improved

Implementation relates to the manner and extent to which approaches are implemented and applied within an organization. More specifically, implementation focuses on the extent to which the approach is

- ✓ Implemented with consistency
- ✓ Implemented in all areas and work groups
- ✓ Monitored and continually improved

Outcomes (Category 7) refer to outcomes and achievements. The focus is on

- ✓ Documented outcomes and achievements
- ✓ Assessments of current performance
- ✓ Examination of improvement trends over time

Institution, Department, or Program Overview

    0.1 Mission, Structure, and Workforce
    0.2 Programs, Services, and Constituencies
    0.3 Peers and Leaders
    0.4 Challenges and Opportunities

1: Leadership

    1.1 Organizational Leadership
    1.2 Public and Professional Leadership Activities
    1.3 Ethics and Social Responsibility

2: Purposes and Plans

    2.1 Plan Development
    2.2 Plan Implementation

3: Beneficiary and Constituency Relationships

    3.1 Needs and Expectations
    3.2 Relationship Enhancement

4: Programs and Services

    4.1 Mission-Critical Programs, Services, and Processes
    4.2 Operational and Support Services and Associated Processes

5: Faculty/Staff and Workplace

    5.1 Faculty and Staff
    5.2 Workplace

6: Metrics, Assessment, and Analysis

    6.1 Assessment Approach and Methods
    6.2 Comparative Analysis
    6.3 Information Sharing and Use

7: Outcomes and Achievements

    7.1 Leadership
    7.2 Purposes and Plans
    7.3 Beneficiary and Constituency Relationships
    7.4 Programs and Services
    7.5 Faculty/Staff and Workplace
    7.6 Metrics, Assessment, and Analysis

FIGURE W.1. Excellence in Higher Education framework.

  ✓ Performance indicators and measures that link to the mission, vision, plans, and goals
  ✓ Comparisons with peers, aspirants, and leading organizations

Percentage Ratings

For each category, *approach*, *implementation*, and *outcomes* are rated 0% to 100%. At one end of the continuum is a rating of 100%, which would be appropriate if *all* of the criteria set forth in a particular category were fully addressed, such that the organization is "the best anywhere"—an international leader—in this area. At the other extreme, a 0% would be appropriate if the organization has not addressed any of the criteria in the category.

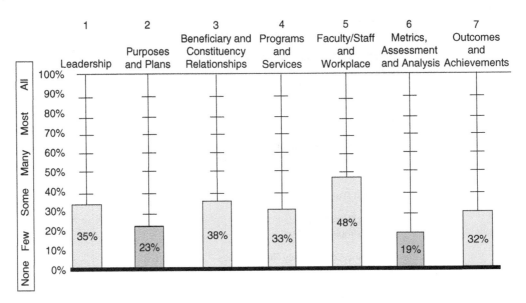

FIGURE W.2. Sample EHE profile.

"Form A: Percentage Rating Guide" (see p. 124) provides a detailed description of the percentage scoring ranges and their interpretation.

Unlike the assessment scale familiar to most educators, 50% or 60% are not "failing" ratings in the EHE or Baldrige frameworks. Rather, as described in Form A, these middle-range ratings are used to characterize organizations with reasonably successful approaches and implementation strategies and results. Such ratings also indicate that there is additional room for improvement.

Forms are provided in the Forms and Guides section for recording percentage ratings for each category. The average rating for each category can be recorded on Form I. When the rating process is complete, the result is a profile such as that illustrated in the sample profile (Figure W.2). The rating distribution tables and bar charts may be completed manually using these forms or with the Ratings Calculator application provided as a part of the *Facilitator's Materials*.

For each category illustrated in Figure W.2, the rating process is completed as follows:

1. Individuals participating in the evaluation process select the percentage rating that in their judgment best corresponds to the extent of *approach* and *implementation* by the organization being reviewed for each category. *Outcomes*, rather than approach and implementation, are the focus for ratings in Category 7.
2. The average percentage awarded by all raters is calculated, and that average is recorded on the form for that category and also entered in the Summary Rating Chart (Form I). Calculations[1] can be completed either manually or using the Ratings Calculator provided in the *Facilitator's Materials*.

If the manual calculation option is selected, Forms B to H are used to record and calculate the average percentage ratings for each category. The chart provided on Form I is used to record the summary of ratings across all categories.

Note

---

1. Unlike the EHE process, the Baldrige scoring methodology also incorporates the allocation of points for each category and arrives at a total score across all categories by multiplying the number of points available in each category by the average percentage rating. This approach has the effect of weighting some categories more than others. Organizations that intend to prepare a Baldrige submission should investigate the details of this process (www.nist.gov/baldrige).

Forms and Guides

THE FOLLOWING SECTION PROVIDES a detailed description of the rating process, along with forms, for those who want to include this activity as part of the assessment process.

Form A: Percentage Rating Guide

Form B: Category 2: Purposes and Plans

Form C: Category 3: Beneficiary and Constituency Relationships

Form D: Category 1: Leadership

Form E: Category 4: Programs and Services

Form F: Category 5: Faculty/Staff and Workplace

Form G: Category 6: Metrics, Assessment, and Analysis

Form H: Category 7: Outcomes and Achievements

Form I: Summary Rating Chart

Form A: Percentage Rating Guide.

Rating	Approach and Implementation	Outcomes
100% to 90%	• A superior approach; systematically addressing **all** dimensions of the category/item. • Fully implemented without significant weakness or gaps in any area. • Widely recognized leader in the category/item. • Systematic approach and commitment to excellence and continuous improvement fully ingrained in the organization and its culture.	• Exceptional, documented, current, and sustained outcomes and achievements related to the mission, vision, and goals and for leadership, purposes and plans, beneficiary and constituency relationships, programs and services, faculty/staff and workplace, and metrics, assessment, and analysis. • Clear and documented evidence that the institution, department, or program is a leader in higher education and more generally.
80% to 70%	• A well-developed, systematic, tested, and refined approach in **most** areas, addressing **most** dimensions of the category. • A fact-based assessment and improvement process throughout **most** of the organization with few significant gaps. • Innovative; recognized as a leader in the category/item. • Clear evidence of excellence and continuous improvement throughout **most** of the organization and its culture.	• Favorable, documented, current, and sustained outcomes and achievements in **most** areas related to the mission, vision, and goals and for leadership, purposes and plans, beneficiary and constituency relationships, programs and services, faculty/staff and workplace, and metrics, assessment and analysis. • Current outcomes and trends are evaluated against—and compare favorably with—peer, competitor, and leading organizations.
60% to 50%	• An effective, systematic approach, responsive to **many** dimensions of the category/item. • The approach is well implemented in **many** areas, although there may be unevenness and inconsistency in particular work groups. • A fact-based, systematic process in place for evaluating and improving effectiveness and efficiency in **many** areas. • Clear evidence of excellence and continuous improvement in **many** areas of the organization and its culture.	• Favorable, documented, current, and sustained outcomes and achievements for **many** areas related to the mission, vision, and goals, and other EHE categories. • **Many** current and sustained outcomes and achievements are evaluated against—and compare favorably with—peer, competitor, and leading organizations. • No pattern of poor outcomes or adverse trends in key areas.
40% to 30%	• An effective, systematic approach, responsive to **some** dimensions of the category/item. • The approach is implemented in **some** areas, but some work units are in the early stages of implementation. • A systematic approach to assessing and improving effectiveness and efficiency in **some** areas. • Clear evidence of excellence and continuous improvement in **some** areas of the organization and its culture.	• Favorable, documented, current, and sustained outcomes and achievements in **some** areas related to the mission, vision, and goals and other EHE categories. • Early stages of developing trends and obtaining comparative information in **some** areas.
20% to 10%	• The beginning of a systematic approach to basic purposes of the category/item. • Category criteria are addressed in **a few** programs, services, activities, and processes. • Major implementation gaps exist that inhibit progress in achieving the basic purpose of the category/item. • Clear evidence of excellence and continuous improvement in **a few** areas of the organization and its culture.	• Outcomes and achievements are documented in **a few** areas related to the mission, vision, and goals and other EHE categories. • Evidence of positive results and improvements in **a few** areas. • Minimal trend or comparative information.
0%	• **No systematic** approach to category/items; anecdotal information on approach and implementation not part of the culture of the organization.	• **No** documented results or poor results. • **No** documented comparisons.

Form B: Category 2: Purposes and Plans.

2: Purposes and Plans

Rating

0%	10%	20%	30%	40%	50%	60%	70%	80%	90%	100%

_____ / _____ = _____
Weighted   #   Average
Total   Voting   %

Form C: Category 3: Beneficiary and Constituency Relationships.

3: Beneficiary and Constituency Relationships

Rating

0%	10%	20%	30%	40%	50%	60%	70%	80%	90%	100%

_____ / _____ = _____
Weighted   #   Average
Total   Voting   %

Form D: Category 1: Leadership.

1: Leadership

Rating

0%	10%	20%	30%	40%	50%	60%	70%	80%	90%	100%

_____   /   _____   =   _____

Weighted   #   Average
Total   Voting   %

Form E: Category 4: Programs and Services.

4: Programs and Services

Rating

0%	10%	20%	30%	40%	50%	60%	70%	80%	90%	100%

_____   /   _____   =   _____

Weighted   #   Average
Total   Voting   %

Form F: Category 5: Faculty/Staff and Workplace.

5: Faculty/Staff and Workplace

Rating

0%	10%	20%	30%	40%	50%	60%	70%	80%	90%	100%

_____ / _____ = _____
Weighted   #   Average
 Total   Voting   %

Form G: Category 6: Metrics, Assessment, and Analysis.

6: Metrics, Assessment, and Analysis

Rating

0%	10%	20%	30%	40%	50%	60%	70%	80%	90%	100%

_____ / _____ = _____
Weighted   #   Average
 Total   Voting   %

Form H: Category 7: Outcomes and Achievements.

7: Outcomes and Achievements

Rating

0%	10%	20%	30%	40%	50%	60%	70%	80%	90%	100%

_____ / _____ = _____
Weighted   #   Average
Total   Voting   %

Form I: Summary Rating Chart.

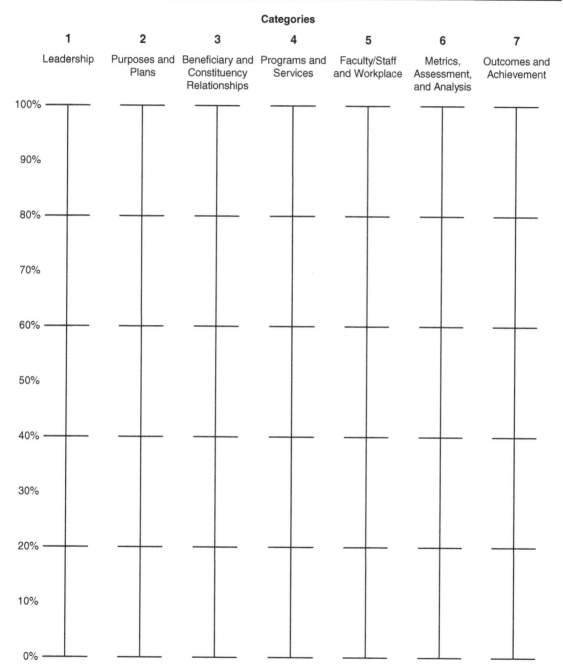

For Product Safety Concerns and Information please contact our EU
representative GPSR@taylorandfrancis.com Taylor & Francis Verlag GmbH,
Kaufingerstraße 24, 80331 München, Germany

Printed and bound by CPI Group (UK) Ltd, Croydon, CR0 4YY
08/06/2025
01897013-0001